Company Dighton Furnace

The Winthrop Wrought Iron Hot Air Furnace for Public and Private Buildings

Company Dighton Furnace

The Winthrop Wrought Iron Hot Air Furnace for Public and Private Buildings

ISBN/EAN: 9783337321024

Printed in Europe, USA, Canada, Australia, Japan

Cover: Foto ©ninafisch / pixelio.de

More available books at **www.hansebooks.com**

THE

WINTHROP

Wrought Iron

HOT AIR FURNACE,

FOR

PUBLIC AND PRIVATE BUILDINGS.

Manufactured only by

Dighton Furnace Company,

NORTH DIGHTON, MASS.

SALESROOMS:

96 & 98 NORTH STREET, BOSTON.

Press of C. A. HACK & SON, Taunton, Mass.

WINTHROP
Wrought Iron Hot Air Furnace.

WINTHROP PORTABLE FURNACE.
FIVE SIZES.

No. 2, Diam. of Fire Pot, (inside of Lining)		16 in.	Price,	$110.
No. 3,	"	"	19 "	"	130.
No. 4,	"	"	22 "	"	160.
No. 5,	"	"	25 "	"	190.
No. 6,	"	"	28 "	"	240.

THE
WINTHROP HEATER.

SECTIONAL VIEW OF THE WINTHROP.

SHOWING THE DIRECTION OF DRAFT.

Diam. of Radiator—No 2,	25 in.
" " " 3,	28 "
" " " 4,	31 "
" " " 5,	34 "
" " " 6,	40 "

THE

Winthrop Wrought Iron Furnace,

FOR SETTING IN BRICK.

THE WINTHROP BRICK SET FURNACE.

Four Sizes.

No. 3,	. . . . .	Price, $120.
" 4,	. . . .	" 150.
" 5,	. . . .	" 180.
" 6,	. . . .	" 225.

Diameter of Fire Pot, same as in the Portable.

Covering Bars, $10.00 per set, extra.

Prefatory Remarks.

Thousands of people are slowly poisoning themselves by breathing impure air in their houses, in consequence of improper heating arrangements. Red hot stoves and furnaces account for the increase of sickness in so many families during the winter season, and a thousand ailments with which people are afflicted would be kept from the door, if proper attention was given to the warming and ventilating of our dwellings. It is too often the case that in building our houses, we study carefully to have everything convenient and well arranged, but scarcely give a thought to the most important thing, of having pure air to breath during the large portion of the year, when the house must be closed and warmth supplied by artificial means.

A Cast Iron Furnace with numberless pipes and joints, though it may heat your house sufficiently, yet it cannot be put together so tight but that it will allow more or less escape of gas, poisoning the air, and bringing in its train disease and death ; add to this, red hot cast iron plates over which the air as it comes through the furnace passes, and you need not wonder that the physician has to spend a large portion of the winter in ministering to the ailments of your family.

It has been found that the only way to secure perfect freedom from a leakage of gas, and the annoyance of dust, in a Furnace, is by having it made of Wrought Iron, riveted together as tight as a steam boiler. It has also been found by actual experiments that Wrought Iron is not open to the objections which can be brought against Cast Iron as a heat radiator. With a perfectly tight Wrought Iron Radiator, and a Fire Chamber lined with brick, we secure everything requisite to furnish pure warm air and freedom from all poisonous gases.

In the construction of the Winthrop Wrought Iron Furnace, due regard has been had to Health, Economy, and Perfect Operation; and we call your attention to an investigation of this Furnace, confidently believing it to be superior to any heating apparatus now before the public. Several eminent Physicians are using the Winthrop Furnace and speak of it in the highest terms of praise, and in no single instance where it has been used has it failed to give entire satisfaction. A large number of churches and school houses are warmed by the Winthrop Furnace, and in every case perfectly satisfactory as to quality and quantity of heat supplied, as well as economy in the consumption of fuel.

The Wrought Iron Radiator of the Winthrop Furnace is made by a practical boiler maker and is riveted perfectly tight, so that there can be no possible escape of gas, or dust into the hot air chambers. There are no pipes with cemented joints, from which the gas is liable to escape, but everything is tight, and all poisonous gases pass off through the smoke pipe.

To secure durability, the lower section of the Furnace enclosing the fire pot is made of Cast Iron, experience having proved that ashes and soot which accumulate at the bottom of a Furnace will not act on cast iron as readily as upon Wrought Iron ; Cast Iron lasting much longer.

The Fire Pot is a Cast Iron cylinder lined with fire-brick of the best quality, thus securing a mild, and perfectly health-ful heat uncontaminated by contact with red hot plates. With this arrangement for burning coal we consider the use of a water evaporator entirely unnecessary, but an evapo-rator is furnished in all cases when desired.

By a peculiar arrangement of the flues, found in no other furnace, we secure in the Winthrop Furnace the best results from the combustion of fuel, and the largest possible amount of radiating surface ; for quickness of operation it is unex-celled, and the large radiating surface utilized, combined with the double casing, prevents the escape of heat into the chimney and cellar.

The arrangement of the grate is such that it can be re-moved when necessary, and a new one put in without dis-turbing the linings.

Every furnace should be thoroughly cleaned out at the close of the season, but it is the case with most furnaces that this is a difficult thing to do, the base of the furnace being so complicated as to render it impossible to get at it in all its parts. This trouble has been thoroughly overcome in the Winthrop, every part of the base being accessible so that it may be thoroughly cleaned.

The Winthrop Wrought Iron Furnace is the result of close observation and careful study, and in presenting it to the public we do so with full confidence in its merits. It has been thoroughly tried under various circumstances, and has been pronounced by practical furnace men to be the beŝt furnace they have seen. In its mechanical construction it is unsurpassed, being made of the best material, and by experienced workmen ; and we guarrantee satisfaction in every respect to all who make a trial of this furnace.

Much has been written about the permeability to poisonous gases of wrought and cast iron. Scientific men have asserted that gases will pass freely through the pores of cast iron, while wrought iron is exempt from this objection, while on the other hand, scientific men have asserted that one is no more permeable to gas than the other. Where doctors disagree we shall not attempt to decide, but there is one point upon which all sensible men can be agreed, viz: that a Wrought Iron Furnace riveted as tight as a steam boiler guarantees a freedom from the escape of gas and dust which cannot be attained by a cast iron furnace with its many joints however closely they may be bolted and cemented.

Recommendations.

We call your attention to the following testimonials from a few of those who are using the Winthrop furnace. Many more could be given but we consider these enough, and we would without hesitation refer to any one who has used the Winthrop, confident that they will give a good report.

Office of T. H. & W. H. WHITE, }
Dealers in Stoves, Furnaces, &c. }

Barre, Mass., April 10th, 1874.

DIGHTON FURNACE CO. *Gentlemen:*

After I had made my mind up to warm my house with some kind of a Furnace, I took quite a while among furnace dealers before I · made a purchase for myself. My wife had been for a number of years troubled with weak lungs, and it was feared by us all that the change would not be beneficial, but we concluded to try it, as we could go back to stoves again if it should be found to be for her good. Being a dealer in Furnaces, with no other man in the trade in town,

I could buy of any man the Furnace I found best to my mind, and I could find none I liked as well as the Winthrop.

I had it put up with good sized pipes, and registers well balanced for distance, to the rooms I wanted to warm, which were four on the first floor and two up stairs. We started the fire Nov. 1st and up to April 1st have used just 6,900 lbs. of coal. We had the house warm both night and day, and it is quite exposed, no house being on either side, standing alone on one side of the street, but not a large house. The effect upon the health of my family has been very gratifying. The house being warm all over, with *pure air, no dust, gas* or smoke at any time, enabled my wife to go from one room to another about her work without breathing cold air, which always made her cough. She says she cannot remember when she has been so free from a cold or chills as during the past winter. In fact, we like it; would not part with it, and have no desire to go back to stoves, or change furnaces.

Yours respectfully,

T. H. WHITE.

Bangor, April 27, 1874.

DIGHTON FURNACE CO. *Gentlemen:*

I have thoroughly tested your " Winthrop " Wrought Iron Furnace the past winter, and do not hesitate to say, that in my opinion it is in every respect everything it is recommended. I consider its construction superior to any Furnace in the market. The fire pot is larger than that of any Furnace I have seen, thereby bringing the fire in close contact with the dome. The screen or partition over the pot, that sends the fire to the front of the Furnace I consider a great improvement. Together with the sifting chamber, grate, and tin lining, make it as near a perfect heater as Furnaces can well be.

Yours, respectfully,

W. H. PRITCHARD.

THE GLOBE PUBLISHING CO., ⎰ .
92 Washington Street. ⎱

Boston, July 1, 1874.

DIGHTON FURNACE COMPANY. *Dear Sirs:*

I take pleasure in stating that the Winthrop Wrought Iron Furnace which I purchased of you gives entire satisfaction. It is free from gas or dust; and is a very economical Furnace, judging by the quantity of coal consumed in heating thoroughly and evenly.

Respectfully yours,

CHAS. H. TAYLOR,
Manager of the Globe.

Bangor, April 26, 1874.

WILLIAM H. PRITCHARD, Esq. *Dear Sir:*

The Winthrop Furnace, No. 4, I procured of you, last Fall, for use at the Almshouse, proved perfectly satisfactory. It burns coal or wood equally well, and is a great heater.

Yours, respectfully,

SAMUEL JEWETT, *Supt. Almshouse.*
Bangor, Maine.

Marblehead, April 11th, 1874.

Messrs. FROTHINGHAM & FIFIELD. *Dear Sirs:*

To your inquiry asking my opinion of the Winthrop Wrought Iron Furnace, I reply that the one which you put into my house Nov. 4th, 1873, has given perfect satisfaction, and is in every particular all that you represent it. The fire which your man kindled when it was set up is still burning, and no particle of kindling wood has since been used to enliven it, although frequently left twenty-four, and sometimes thirty-six hours without attendance. My usual custom, however, is to feed and shake down morning and evening. It has continually heated four rooms directly from registers, and the register in the open hall has kept four other chambers very comfortable. To this time it has consumed $5\frac{1}{2}$ tons of coal, and the ease and simplicity of managing it is remarkable. I think one advantage which this Furnace possesses over most others which I have seen is that it has a larger fire-pot, which enables the user to keep a larger body of coal ignited, and when kept in a smouldering condition produces as much or more heat than a smaller body on which a continual draft is required, and the consumption of fuel is much less.

Respectfully yours,

WILLIAM J. GOLDTHWAIT.

Newport, R. I., July 13, 1874.

DIGHTON FURNACE CO. *Gents:*

The No. 4 Winthrop Wrought Iron Furnace purchased of you last Fall, was bought after a careful examination of most of the leading Furnaces in the market, and I can cheerfully add my testimony in its favor. It has fully equalled my expectations in every respect, and I have yet to see the furnace I would be willing to exchange it for. I have spoken to Mr. H. M. Pray in reference to the one he purchased when I bought mine, and from what he told me, am certain he would endorse the above without reserve.

Very truly yours,

L. R. BLACKMAN.

New Haven, Conn., June 29, 1874.

THOMAS H. BRADY, Esq.,

New Britain Conn.

Dear Sir:

I take great pleasure in saying that the "Winthrop" Wrought Iron Furnace bought of you has proved to be all you recommended. Simple in construction, easily managed, imparting a heat entirely free from *gas*, the atmosphere of my rooms being as mild and pleasant as if heated by steam. I most willingly recommend the *Winthrop.*

Yours, very truly,

EDWARD McCARTY.

Springfield July 15th 1874.

We have used the "Winthrop" Wrought Iron Furnace, sold by D. B. Montague & Co., the last year and will say, after using Furnaces for many years, we never have had one or seen one that was as near perfection, taking all in all, as the "Winthrop." We believe it to be the most durably made, economical in burning coal, and giving the most heat from it, and entirely free from gas, of any in the market.

LINCOLN & LENEY.

Lynn, June 12, 1874.

Messrs. SMITH & POOL. *Gents:*

The No. 4 Winthrop Wrought Iron Furnace had of you, works admirably and gives the best satisfaction, being economical and a great heater, and thoroughly gas tight. Can recommend it in every respect. GEO. H. PLUMMER.

Lynn, July 3, 1874.

Messrs. SMITH & POOL. *Gents:*

It gives us pleasure to testify to the good qualities of the No. 2 Winthrop Wrought Iron Portable Furnace had of you last fall, to heat our store. It works like a charm, being very economical, thoroughly gas tight and easily managed. Can recommend it in every respect. Yours, &c.

PAGE & BAILEY.

Lynn, July, 1874.

Messrs. SMITH & POOL. *Gents:*

The No. 3 Winthrop Wrought Iron Furnace you put in my house

last fall, fully meets the recommendation you gave it, and I am happy to say, after a fair trial that it more than meets my expectations. It is easily managed, economical and gas tight, also a great heater.

Yours, &c.

J. O. GUILD,

52 Johnson St., Lynn.

———

The "Winthrop" Wrought Iron Furnace set for me last year, in my residence, 73 Spring St., by D. B. Montague & Co., just suits me *perfectly in all respects.*

EDWIN DICKINSON,

Com'l Agent Union Paper Co.,

Springfield, Mass.

July 15, 1874.

———

Office of CHARLES H. DEYO,
Dealer in Stoves, Tinware, &c.

No. Brookfield, Mass., July 2, 1874.

Messsrs. DIGHTON FURNACE Co. *Gents :*

The parties using the Winthrop in this place, are :

Liberty Stone, No. 3.

A. O. Blood, No. 3.

Each of them heat five rooms, and give perfect satisfaction.

Yours respectfully,

C. H. DEYO.

Brockton, July 1, 1874.

E. W. HOLMES.   *Dear Sir:*

Having used one of the No. 3 Winthrop Plate Iron Furnaces in my house during the last Winter, I find it to be all you claim as a powerful heater with a small amount of fuel, free from gas and dust easily regulated.   Respectfully yours,

ISAIAH BEAL.

West Medway, Mass., April 29, 1874.

DIGHTON FURNACE CO.   *Gents:*

In reply to yours of 21st inst. I would say, that the Winthrop Wrought Iron Furnaces which I have put up in this place are giving perfect satisfaction in every case.   I am much pleased with the construction and operation of the Furnace.   Yours truly,

OBED RUGGLES.

Brockton, Mass., June, 1874.

Mr. E. W. HOLMES.

The Winthrop Wrought Iron Furnace which you placed in my house has worked to my entire satisfaction.   It is economical, easy to manage and a powerful heater.   I can cheerfully recommend it as a superior Furnace.   Yours, truly,

C. M. HATHAWAY.

Bath, June 19, 1874.

Mr. S. J. WATSON.   *Dear Sir*:

Having used the past Winter a Winthrop Furnace, I certify with pleasure that it worked to my entire satisfaction.   It is a great heater and very easy to manage.   For economy of fuel and convenience of arrangement, I do not think it is surpassed by any other Furnace now in use.   Yours, &c.

GEO. A. PREBLE.

Bath, July 3, 1874.

Mr. S. J. WATSON.   *Dear Sir:*

The Winthrop Furnace you put in my house on trial last Fall, has proved a *success*, heating to our *perfect* satisfaction, and with less fuel. Having had experience with three different Furnaces, I feel it consistent to say that it is the *best*, most *economical*, and less complicated than any I have used.   Very truly,

SAM'L ANDERSON, JR.

Vernon Depot, April 27, 1874.

Mr. T. CHILD, Agt. Dighton Furnace Co.   *Dear Sir:*

I am happy to be able to say that the Winthrop Furnaces placed in the M. E. Church at Niantic, Ct., gives complete satisfaction They were thoroughly tested every day during a protracted series of meetings, lasting about 7 weeks, and never failed us.   Indeed I think

oue of them, (you know we have two), would have comfortably
heated the house any day this winter.

Truly yours,

D. A. JORDAN,

Late Pastor of Niantic M. E. Church.

Hingham, March 5, 1874.

DIGHTON FURNACE Co.   *Sirs:*

The Furnace that you put in my house last Fall has worked well
in every respect. It has supplied the heat of two coal stoves, and
one air tight in former winters, and has used no more coal than did
the two stoves.   Yours, &c.

H. E. SPALDING, M. D.

Barre, Mass., April 30, 1874.

Messrs. T. H. & W. H. WHITE.   *Gents:*

The Winthrop Hot Air Furnace which you set for me last fall,
pleases me. It is easy to run, giving but little trouble to keep a continuous fire, takes but a small amount of coal, heats up quick, and the
heat is soft and pleasant with no smell of gas or other impurities in
the house. I should not like to part with it.

Yours,

DR. GEO. BROWN.

New Bedford, Mass., May 10, 1874.

DIGHTON FURNACE CO. *Gents:*

In reply to your inquiry we have to state that the Winthrop Wrought Iron Furnaces sold by us in New Bedford are giving entire satisfaction in every case. We hear of no trouble from gas or dust but all testify to the purity and healthfullness of the heat supplied, and the economical operation of the Furnace. We consider them in their construction a superior and very desirable Furnace, and are very much pleased with the arrangement for cleaning out the base.

Respectfully yours,

WOOD, BRIGHTMAN & CO.

First Baptist Church, Rockport, Mass.

Messrs. SMITH & POOL, put into the Baptist Church of Rockport, November last, a No. 5 Winthrop Furnace, and after using it one Winter we are happy to say that it has given entire satisfaction, proving to be all that it was recommended.

JUDSON POOL,
CHARLES POOL, } Committee.
LEVI SANBORN, JR.

Rockport, Mass., May 7, 1874.

Taunton, April, 1874.

Mr. I. B. BRIGGS. *Dear Sir:*

The No. 3 Winthrop Wrought Iron Furnace which you placed in my house last Fall has given me entire satisfaction. It is easily managed, the air pure and soft and does not waste heat in the cellar like other Furnaces. I think it is superior to any in the market.

HENRY S. WASHBURN.

Lynn, Mass., May 9, 1874.

Messrs. SMITH & POOL.   *Gents.*

I have used the Winthrop Wrought Iron Furnace during the past Winter, and am greatly pleased with the construction and operation of it.   The Grate arrangement, is in my opinion superior to any other I have seen.   Very respectfully,

W. A. FAULKNER.

From the Mayor of New Britain, Conn.

DIGHTON FURNACE CO.   *Gentlemen.*

Upon representations of the superiority of the " Winthrop Wrought Iron Furnace, and upon satisfactory examination of one of them in use in one of the churches of this city, I had the said Furnace placed in my dwelling house, in Dec. 1873.   It was in constant use during the Winter, and afforded a most agreeable heat, without gas, and with marked economy in the consumption of coal.   This Furnace is easily managed, and in every respect it has given me entire satisfaction.   Yours truly,

S. W. HART.

Rockport, May 7th, 1874.

Messrs. SMITH & POOL.   *Gents:*

The Winthrop Furnace set in my house by you, heats economically, and is but little care.   I like it.

HENRY DENNIS.

Mansfield, Mass., April 23, 1874.

DIGHTON FURNACE CO. *Gents.* .

I am well pleased with the No. 3 Winthrop which you put into my house last Fall, in every respect. My sitting room is a large one 21 × 18 feet, out of which opens a bed room on the north side. I have never yet had occasion to open the register in the bed room as the one in the large room heats both sufficiently. The register in the front hall heats all the chambers sufficiently, four sleeping rooms. I can regulate the Furnace with more ease and less care than I even could a parlor stove, the body of fire being so much larger it will run longer and heat more evenly than any stove. I have kept a continuous fire all winter with a moderate amount of coal, and have had no trouble from gas or dust.   -   Yours truly,

F. G. HODGES.

Taunton, April 15, 1874.

DIGHTON FURNACE CO. *Gents.*

In reply to your inquiry of the 1st, would state that the Winthrop Furnaces sold in Taunton have given perfect satisfaction. We get good reports in every case, have had no trouble or complaint from gas or dust, but all agree and pronounce it the best, and most economical Furnace extant. In my opinion they are the most durable of any Wrought Iron Furnace in the market, being constructed so that *all* soot and ashes can be removed from the base with but little trouble.

I. B. BRIGGS.

Barre, Mass., May 11, 1874.

DIGHTON FURNACE CO.   *Gents.*

In reply to your inquiry, would say the Winthrop Wrought Iron Furnace works finely, is a powerful heater, easy to manage, using but a moderate amount of fuel.   We can with the fullest confidence recommend it to the public, after testing it personally, as a durable and economical Furnace.

T. H. & W. H. WHITE.

Charlestown, Mass., April 29, 1874.

Mr. R. DOWD:

I think the Winthrop Wrought Iron Furnace from its *superior construction*, must be the most durable and perfect of all the Plate Iron Furnaces in market.   Mine has worked well in every respect, no trouble to run it continuously, and the heated air is soft and fine, has kept my house comfortable with a reasonable amount of coal.   I can most cheerfully recommend it.

Z. S. DOANE.

Lynn, Mass., July 3, 1874.

Messrs. SMITH & POOL.   *Gents.*

I have used the Winthrop Wrought Iron Furnace the past year and do not hesitate to recommend it as a good, economical heater, easy to manage, and entirely free from the smell of gas, which I have always found with other furnaces.

PHILIP CHASE.

Medway, Mass., April, 1874.

Mr. O. RUGGLES. *Sir:*

The No. 4 Winthrop Wrought Iron Furnace you set in my brick work last Fall fully answers your description as to heating capacity, economy of fuel, purity of air, and absolute freedom from dust or gas, and its entire arrangement is such that it is very easily taken care of. I can freely commend it as being the best Furnace I ever used.

P. S. You can use this in any way that will be a benefit to the general public. Truly yours,

ALEX. L. B. MONROE, M. D.

———————————

Taunton, April 14, 1874.

DIGHTON FURNACE CO. *Gents:*

I have used the past Winter a No. 4 Winthrop Wrought Iron Furnace to heat my house. I have had no trouble in warming sufficiently 6 large rooms in the coldest weather with a moderate amount of coal, and is easily regulated for mild weather. It gives perfect satisfaction, and we have had entire freedom from gas and dust.

L. J. WILMARTH.

———————————

Lynn, July 27, 1874.

Messrs. SMITH & POOL. *Gents.*

The Furnace I purchased of you a year ago, has proved itself in every respect all you claimed it to be. I would cheerfully recommend to any one wishing a house *thoroughly heated*, to purchase the Winthrop Furnace.   Yours truly,

                                        S. B. VALPEY.

————————————

                                        Taunton, June 24, 1874.

DIGHTON FURNACE CO.   *Gentlemen:*

I have been repeatedly solicited to give my opinion in regard to the Winthrop Wrought Iron Furnace manufactured by you, and put into my house by Mr. I. B. Briggs of this city, and I deem it but justice to you to state that I consider it the very best Furnace yet produced. As regards economy in the consumption of fuel, ease of management, freedom from dust and coal gas (the greatest of all annoyances in Hot Air Furnaces), and durability and simplicity of construction, it is all that can be desired. I would advise any one contemplating putting in a heating apparatus to give the Winthrop an impartial examination before purchasing.

                    Very truly yours,
                      HENRY S. HACK,
                        Of C. A. Hack & Son, Printers.

We append the names of some of the parties using the
WINTHROP WROUGHT IRON FURNACE, to any of whom we re-
fer for further information as to the practical operation of the
Furnace.

Chas. H. Taylor, - - -	Boston,
S. G. Parsons, - -	"
G. B. Outen, - - - -	"
I. B. Patten, - - -	"
C. Blake, - - - -	"
Geo. T. McLauthlin, - -	"
Stratton & Plimpton, - -	"
T. C. Newcomb, - - -	"
C. F. Newcomb, - - -	"
E. F. Snow, - - - -	Harrison Square.
Arlington Piano Co., - -	Leominster.
Geo. Daman, - - - -	"
S. Bucknam, - - - -	Portland, Me.
W. C. Fowler, - - -	Everett, Mass.
J. H. Whitman, - - -	" "
Dr. H. E. Spaulding, - -	Hingham, "
David Cushing, 2nd, - - -	" "
Baptist Church, - - -	Edgartown, "
M. E. Church, - - - -	Brookline "
M. E. Church, - - -	Niantic, Ct.
Dr. H. C. Kendrick. - - -	Lancaster, Mass.
C. H. Chase, - - - -	Clinton, "
M. E. Church, - - - -	Somerset, "
J. Y. McClintock, - - -	Belfast, Me.
Miles S. Staples, - - -	" "
Parker Lawrence, - - -	Lynn, Mass.
Philip Chase, - - - -	" "

Dr. M. J. Flanders, - -	Lynn, Mass.
J. O. Guild, - - - -	" "
Page & Bailey, - - -	" "
Wm. A. Faulkner, - - -	" "
S. B. Valpey, - - -	" "
John Shaw, 2d, - - - -	" "
Geo. H. Plummer, - -	" "
C. H. Ramsdell, - - -	" "
Baptist Church, - - -	Rockport, Mass.(No. 5)
Henry Dennis, - - -	" "
Joshua Farr, - - -	" "
Winthrop Thurston, - - -	" "
Capt. Wm. Flye, - - -	Topsham, Me.
Liberty Stone, - - - -	No. Brookfield, Mass.
A. O. Blood, - - -	✔ " "
John Brooks, - . - -	Arlington, "
C. M. Hatch, - - -	Brighton, "
Geo. Clark, - - - -	Sherburn, "
F. G. Hodges, - - -	Mansfield, "
Benjamin Anthony, - - -	New Bedford, Mass.
Noah Tripp, - - - -	" "
John McCullough, - - -	" "
Oliver Read, - - - -	Newport, R. I.
Commodore W. B. Edgar, -	" "
Anthony Stuart, Jr., - -	" "
Adams House, oc'pi'd by T.A. Vyse,	" "
Chas. G. Muenchinger, - -	" "
Gen. J. N. Palmer, - - -	" "
H. W. Pray, - - - -	" "
Wm. M. Steadman, - - -	" "
L. R. Blackman, - - -	" "

Wm. L. Kinsman, -   -   -   Salem, Mass.
Benjamin Fabens, -   -   -   "   "
Wm. J. Goldthwait,   -   -   "   "
Silas B. Winn.   -   -   -   "   "
Winthrop St. Baptist Ch. Parsonage   Taunton, "
Broadway Cong'l Church   "   "   "
L. J. Wilmarth,   -   -   -   "   "
James P. Ellis,   -   -   -   "   "
Alexander Williams,   -   -   "   "
James H. Codding,   -   -   "   "
Charles Curtis, -   -   -   -   "   "
Isaac Washburn, -   -   -   "   "
H. S. Washburn,   -   -   -   "   "
James Rait, -   -   -   -   "   "
Henry S. Hack,   -   -   -   "   "
L. Nichols, -   -   -   -   Fall River, Mass., No. 4.
Children's Home, - -   -   -   "   "   " 5.
W. H. Chase,   -   -   -   "   "   " 3.
N. M. Wood.   -   -   -   -   "   "   " 2.
G. W. Bean, -   -   -   -   "   "   " 2.
Edwin Dickerson,   -   -   .   Springfield, "
Lincoln & Long,   -   -   -   "   "
J. R. Hewitt, -   -   -' -   "   "
Rufus Chase,   -   -   -   "   "
North Church, Salem St., -   -   "   " No. 8&5.
H. S. Newell,   -   -   -   Chicopee, Falls, Mass.
Porter Underwood, -   -   -   Holyoke,   "
A. Street,   -   -   -   -   "   "
G. H. Peck,   -   -   -   Collins Depot, Mass.
H. J. Nelson,   -   -   -   Burlington, Vt.
Geo. S. Hopkins,   -   -   -   Chelsea, Mass.

Parker Lawrence, - - -	Chelsea, Mass.
Wm. B. Lawton, - - -	Warren, R. I.
E. H. Kingman, - - -	Brockton, Mass.
C. M. Hathaway, - - -	" "
Isaiah Beale, - - - -	" " 2 No. 4.
Whitman School House, - -	" " 2 No. 5.
New Jerusalem Church, - -	" "
Capt. Geo. A. Preble, - -	Bath, Me.
Samuel D. Haley, - - -	" "
E. C. Hyde, - - - -	" "
James B. Drake - - -	" "
Sam'l Anderson, Jr., - - -	" "
Mrs. J. P. Morse, - - -	" "
Edward McCarthy - - -	New Haven, Ct.
S. W. Hart, - - - -	New Britain, "
Gen. A. P. Blunt, - - -	Manchester, N. H.
Albert Mead, - - - -	Natick, Mass.
J. O. Hayden, - - - -	Somerville, "
Z. S. Doane, - - - -	Charlestown, "
Samuel Jewett, - - - -	Bangor, Me.
Wm. McLauthlin, - - -	Longwood, Mass.
Rev. Clark Carter, - - -	Lawrence, "
John C. Dow, - - -	" "
J. D. Edson, - - - -	" "
N. Ambrose, - - - -	" "
Roland Winslow, - - -	Jamaica Plain, Mass.
Thomas Mayo, - - -	" " "

In addition to the proper warming of the house, we give special attention to the equally important matter of furnishing a complete cooking apparatus for the kitchen. **THE CONQUEROR COOK STOVE** has been used by hundreds, and has never failed to give complete satisfaction.

We manufacture three sizes of the Conqueror.

Price of No. 7, with Ware
" " 8, " "
" " 9, " "

We also furnish the same with Extension Top and Patent Cast Iron Water Tank.

Price of No. 7, with Ex. Top, &c.,
" " " 8, " " " "
" " " 9, " " " "
Hot Water Back and Couplings.

Many persons prefer a Portable Range to a stove, and to meet this demand we are manufacturing the Conquest Hot Closet Range, which has become so well and favorably known as to require hardly a word of commendation from us. On its own merits it has worked its way into popular favor, and our sales of this range are increasing every year.

We manufacture two sizes of each, with and without ware.

Price of No. 7 Hot Closet Range, without ware,

  "   "   " 8 "   "   "   "   "

  "   "   " 7 Single Oven "   "   "

  "   "   " 8   "   "   "   "   "

Hot Water Front and Couplings.

www.ingramcontent.com/pod-product-compliance
Lightning Source LLC
Chambersburg PA
CBHW021458090426
42739CB00009B/1775